Glendalough
History, Monuments and Legends

With best wishes,

George McClafferty

George McClafferty

Glendalough
History, Monuments and Legends

columba

First published, 2012, by

the columba press

55A Spruce Avenue, Stillorgan Industrial Park,
Blackrock, Co Dublin
www.columba.ie

Design, layout and photography by
Emer O Boyle and Orla O Boyle Callaly
Printed by Nicholson & Bass

ISBN: 978-185607-7743

The author would like to express his gratitude to
The Office of Public Works (OPW) for the usage
of the maps.

For my mother Gertie who was a great golfer and
for Aunty Doreen who was a second mother to me.

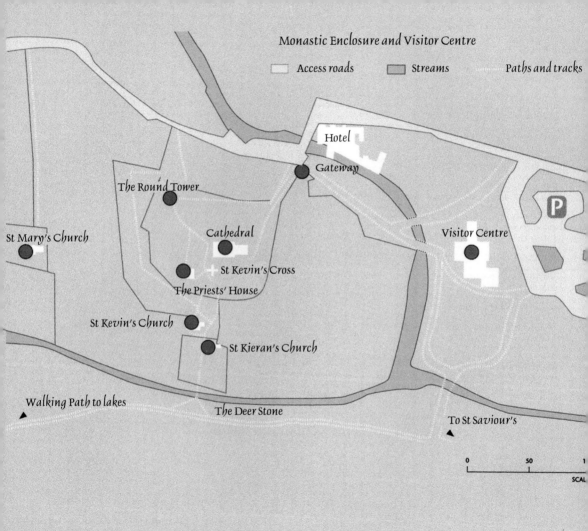

TABLE OF CONTENTS

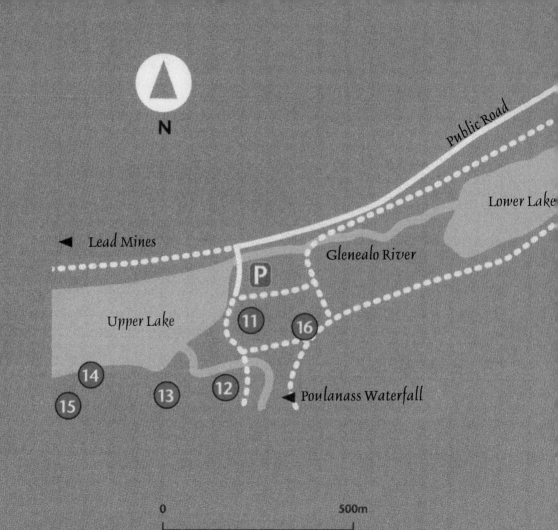

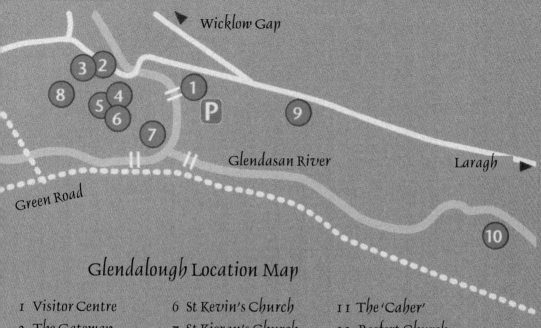

Glendalough Location Map

1 Visitor Centre	6 St Kevin's Church	11 The 'Caher'
2 The Gateway	7 St Kieran's Church	12 Reefert Church
3 The Round Tower	8 St Mary's Church	13 St Kevin's Cell
4 The Cathedral	9 Trinity Church	14 St Kevin's Bed
5 The Priests' House	10 St Saviour's Church	15 Temple-na-skellig
		16 Park Information Office

The Glendalough Valley

Glendalough, with its magnificent natural beauty, is without doubt the best known of the valleys in the Wicklow mountains. Its fame is further enhanced by the extensive early Christian ecclesiastical remains situated at its entrance. The ecclesiastical settlement was founded in the 6th century by St Kevin and flourished here from the 6th to the 12th century as a centre of learning and pilgrimage. Indeed, this tradition of pilgrimage continued well into the 19th century, particularly on June 3rd, St Kevin's feast day. The name, Glendalough, derives from the Irish *Gleann dá Loch* and means 'the valley of the two lakes.'

Running from east to west, the valley is typically U-shaped, broadened and deepened by glacial action. It is bounded to the north by the slopes of Camaderry and to the south by both Lugduff and Derrybawn Mountain. The valley floor is largely occupied by the Upper and Lower Lakes fed mainly by the Glenealo river which tumbles down from the valley head and flows into the western end of the Upper Lake. A second river flowing into the valley is the Lugduff Brook. This little river tumbles down the hill between Lugduff and

Derrybawn Mountain and enters the eastern part of the Upper Lake. Over the past 10,000 years this river has carried over 20 million tonnes of sand and mud down into the lake. The alluvial fan which this has created, has spread right across, dividing the one original lake into two separate lakes. The main ecclesiastical enclosure is located at the entrance to the valley on a bank of sand and gravel which stands some seven metres above the surrounding land. This was a river delta formed when the valley held only one lake and had a higher level than today.

The granite rock at the head of the valley contains veins of mineral quartz with variable amounts of lead and copper sulphides. Between 1800, and 1880 these ores were mined and hundreds of people earned a living extracting the ore from the mine tunnels and surface workings. Up until 1826 a charcoal-fired smelting furnace which used huge amounts of local wood was located at the head of the valley. The mine was abandoned in 1880, but was opened again in 1917, when the demand for lead during World War I resulted in the Foxrock lode being reopened with a grant of £2,500 from the British Ministry of Munitions. Once the war ended, this support was withdrawn and the mines closed again. Visitors to the valley in the 1840s record that most of the trees had been chopped down to be converted into charcoal and that Glendalough was virtually bare, with hardly a tree left standing. Today, many of the trees you can see were planted in the 1850s by the Mining Company of Ireland while, overlooking the valley, commercial plantations of Sitka Spruce and Lodgepole Pine were planted during the 20th century.

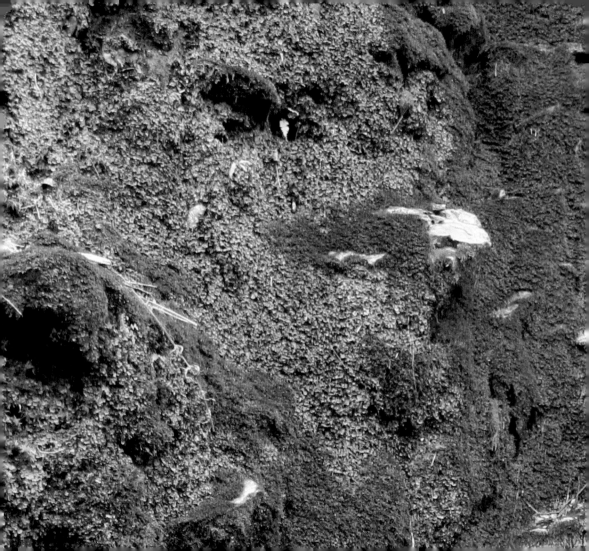

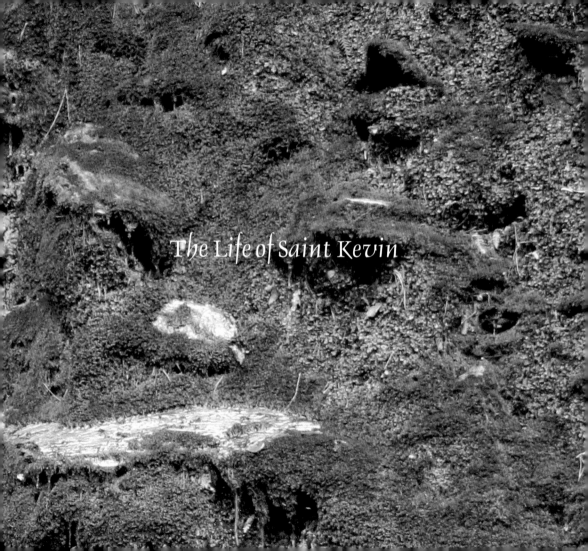

The Life of Saint Kevin

Historically, very little is known about St Kevin. Even the date of his death is uncertain and it is variously recorded in the Annals under the year 618 as well as 622. Clearly both of these were subsequent calculations by the writers of the Annals and are regarded by scholars as dubious. The Irish Martyrologies, calendars of Irish saints, mark Kevin's feast day as June 3rd. The metrical Martyrology of Oengus, which was written about the year AD800, commemorates St Kevin with the following words:

> A soldier of Christ into the land of Ireland
> A high name over wave and sea
> Kevin the holy fair warrior
> In the valley of the two broad lakes.

Three versions of the 'Life of St Kevin' are recorded in Irish and three variations of a single 'Life' in Latin exist in manuscript form. The Latin 'Life' is the earliest and is also considered to be the most reliable. It could originally have been written as early as the year 800. The finest version of it is to be found in the *Codex Kilkenniensis* which is housed in Marsh's Library in Dublin.

There seems to be no direct connection between the Latin and Irish versions of St Kevin's 'Life'. Two of the Irish 'Lives' are in manuscripts housed in Brussels and

were transcribed in the 17th century. The third Irish 'Life' is in manuscripts housed in Dublin and was transcribed in the 18th century. Both the Latin and Irish 'Lives' contain but a few possible truths which are linked together by elaborate accounts of miracles from his baptism by an angel to his fight with the demons in the air shortly before his death. The following account is based on the Latin 'Life'.

Kevin came from the Leinster sept called Dál Messin Corb. His father, who was descended from a Leinster King, was called Coemlug while his mother, Coemall, was also of noble birth. An angel appeared to Coemall, in her sleep, telling her that she would give birth to a son called Coemghan (Kevin) and that he would be father over many monks and be dear to both God and men.

When the child was born, he was sent to be baptised by St Crónán but on the way the party was stopped by a young man who blessed the infant and called him Kevin which means 'fair-begotten'. When the party finally reached Crónán, the holy man enquired of them if they had met anybody on their journey. When they told him about meeting the young man, Crónán recognised that the man was in fact an Angel of the Lord and he then prayed over and blessed the infant.

While Kevin was still an infant, a white cow miraculously arrived at his parents' house each morning and evening and provided two large vessels of milk which were used to nourish the child. As a boy, Kevin was employed by his parents herding sheep. One day, some poor people came to the boy asking for alms. Kevin felt sorry

for them and gave them four of his parents' sheep but miraculously that evening when the sheep were counted none was found to be missing as God wished to reward the boy's charity and save him from any blame.

As a youth, Kevin was placed under the direction of three holy men called Eoghan, Lochan and Éanna. One day, while working with the brethren of the monastery, he was noticed by a young maiden who developed a particular affection for him. The girl made several advances towards Kevin but he rejected them. On one occasion, the girl followed him into a wood and proceeded to tempt him away from the holy life which he had choosen to follow. Kevin picked a bunch of stinging nettles and struck her several times with them in the face and on the arms and legs. The girl, who was severely stung, fell to her knees and implored the young saint's forgiveness. Kevin offered up his prayers for her and afterwards she promised to dedicate her virginity to God. Subsequently, the maiden became distinguished for great prudence and sanctity.

Kevin achieved some fame as a result of this and other miracles which he performed. Greatly displeased at this fame, he stole away and searched for some place where he could live the life of a hermit. During his wanderings, he came upon Glendalough, a beautiful valley in the midst of the mountains with two lakes and a number of clear streams. Kevin decided to stay in the valley and he spent some time dwelling in the hollow of a tree and living on wild herbs and a little water. A local farmer who grazed his cattle in the valley, noticed that one of the animals gave an

almost incredible quantity of milk. He had the cow followed and found that each day the cow made her way to the hollow in the tree and licked Kevin's garments with her tongue. News of this miracle soon reached Eoghan's monastery and Kevin was forced, under protest, to return.

Soon, Kevin left Eoghan's monastery for good and came under the care of Bishop Lugidus who ordained him and sent him with a group of monks to found a monastery at a place called *Cluain Duach*. Although Kevin consented to remain there for some time, and appointed as monks many of the men who flocked to him, he retained the strong desire to live the life of a hermit. Finally, when the monastery was well established, Kevin committed it to the care of his trained men and retired once more to Glendalough.

Here, Kevin founded a monastery in the lower part of the valley where the two clear rivers meet. Having established it, he left it in the care of others and went alone to live in the upper part of the valley where he built a small dwelling on a narrow strip of land and ordered his monks that he should be left alone. Kevin spent seven years living in different places in this part of the valley. Every night, he stood in the cold waters of the Upper Lake and prayed for an hour. A horrible monster in the form of a serpent which dwelt in the lake used to coil itself around the saint, biting and stinging him but it did him no harm such was the fervour of his prayer.

One year, during the season of Lent, when he was living in the cave overlooking the Upper Lake (known today as St Kevin's Bed), he was visited by an angel who told him that a rock overhanging the cave was about to fall on to the cave but Kevin refused to leave the cave until the season of Lent had finished. When Lent was over, the angel returned and told Kevin to follow him. They passed with dry feet across the lake and suddenly the rock fell on the cave as the angel had foretold.

At the end of the seven years, God sent another angel to Kevin who told him to return to the area to the east of the Lower Lake where he was to build a monastery. Kevin did so and said, 'In this place, a great city will spring up in which my resurrection will be'.

Kevin continued to live at Glendalough until his death, when, amidst the tears and lamentations of his monks, he received the most sacred body and blood of Christ from the hands of St Mocherog, a Briton, who had a cell to the east of Kevin's great monastery. Having lived for a period of one hundred and twenty years, he departed this life to join the choirs of angels and archangels in the heavenly Jerusalem.

It is clear that the content of the Lives of St Kevin cannot be taken as historical fact. There are a number of questions which arise from what we are told. First of all, there is no historical evidence to prove the claim that Kevin was descended from the dynasty of Dál Messin Corb. Secondly, the Latin 'Life' tells us that Kevin founded his monastery at the place where the two clear rivers meet which could only be at the entrance to the valley and the place where the Round Tower and Cathedral now stand. The exact location of where the original monastery was founded is the subject of much scholarly dispute with some scholars claiming that it was near the Upper Lake while others argue that it was to the east of the Lower Lake. Finally, it is improbable that Kevin actually lived to the great age of one hundred and twenty years as is claimed in the Latin 'Life' although it is probable that he lived to be quite old.

Glendalough after Saint Kevin

There is a tradition that following the death of Kevin, the monastery was taken over by his nephew Molibba, who, it is said, became the second abbot and first Bishop of Glendalough. However, there is no historical evidence to support this tradition and it may have been a later fabrication to show the continuation of the Dál Messin Corb, the alleged ancestral lineage of the founder saint.

Little is known of Glendalough during the 7th century and existing records do not clearly indicate to which septs or families the earlier abbots and bishops belonged. Ecclesiastical settlements were often founded on lands donated by ruling families from whose ranks came the abbots and their successors. It is possible that the local sept was the Dál Messin Corb and that they held the abbacy of Glendalough during the 7th century. There are a few references in the Annals to the deaths of ecclesiastics at Glendalough during the late 7th century but little else is known of the settlement.

The abbacy of Glendalough certainly seems to have been controlled by the Uí Máil (from whom the Glen of Imaal takes its name) during the 8th century. The ecclesiastical settlement was destroyed by fire in 775 but it is not clear whether the fire was accidental or the result of a hostile attack. The importance of Glendalough as a place of pilgrimage is evident from the references in the Annals to the deaths of a number of important people there. In the year 790, the bones of St Kevin were disinterred and enshrined at the site.

According to the Latin 'Life' of St Kevin, seven visits to Glendalough carried the same benefit as one pilgrimage to Rome.

At around the turn of the 9th century, the dynasty of Uí Dúnlainge became the dominant influence at Glendalough. There are many references in the Annals to the deaths of abbots during this period which indicate that the monastery was very important and wealthy. An entry in the Martyrology of Oengus describes Glendalough as follows:

> *The fortress of Eamhain Macha has vanished*
> *Except that its stones remain*
> *The monastic city of the western world*
> *Is Glendalough of the assemblies.*

The relative peace of the Irish ecclesiastical settlements was shattered with the arrival of the Vikings and Glendalough was plundered by them in 833. They returned and burned a church just two years later. The next fifty years seems to have been fairly peaceful but the Vikings returned in 886 and plundered the site once again.

During the 10th century, the ecclesiastical settlement seems to have been under the control of septs from West Leinster. Most of the stone buildings which survive today date from between this period and the 12th century, as the earlier ecclesiastical structures which were built of perishable materials were gradually replaced by stone edifices. It was during this period that the monastic school was at its height and attracted students from all over Britain, as well as some from other parts of Europe.

Archaeological excavation of contemporary settlements has shown that corn was the main crop while cattle, sheep, pigs and goats were kept. Vegetables and herbs were grown, beehives provided honey and the local rivers and lakes supplied fish. The diet varied from place to place, depending on the wealth and location of the settlement while fasting at certain times was a feature of all ecclesiastical settlements. Both the domestic and farm buildings were built of perishable materials which were easily burnt and needed frequent replacement.

The Uí Muiredaig sept became the dominant influence at Glendalough during the late 10th century and remained there for most of the period up to the middle of the 13th century when record of the abbacy ends. In 1017, 1020 and again in 1061, the settlement was destroyed by fire. These fires were probably accidental but destructive enough to have been recorded in the Annals. In 1043, the site was attacked by a rival sept and sixty inhabitants of the ecclesiastical settlement were slaughtered.

The O'Toole family, a branch of the Uí Muiredaig, succeeded to the abbacy of Glendalough in 1106 when Gilla Comgaill filled the vacant position. At the Synod of Raith Bresail in 1111, the bishopric of Glendalough was reconstituted as a territorial diocese which covered most of modern county Wicklow as well as parts of Kildare and Dublin. Gilla Comgaill's grandson Laurence (Lorcán), who was born about the year 1128, became the second saint associated with Glendalough. As a child, St Laurence O'Toole, lived as a hostage of Dermot MacMurrough, King of Leinster, at Ferns in county Wexford. As a hostage, he was harshly treated and following protests from his father, he was given into the care of the Bishop of Glendalough. Soon, he became attracted to the monastic way of life and he relinquished all claims to the family inheritance. In 1153, he was chosen as Abbot of Glendalough but we are told that he declined the honour of bishop.

Laurence continued as Abbot for the following nine years and much of the 12th century building at Glendalough is attributed to him. Laurence was appointed Archbishop of Dublin in 1162 but frequently returned to Glendalough to spend the season of Lent in the cave known as St Kevin's Bed. As Archbishop of Dublin,

Laurence negotiated between Strongbow and the citizens of Dublin during the siege of 1171. He also helped to negotiate the Treaty of Windsor between Rory O'Connor and Henry II of England in 1175. In 1176, Glendalough was plundered by Anglo-Norman adventurers and in the following year an astonishing flood ran through the settlement taking with it a bridge and mills and leaving fish in the midst of the site.

Laurence was apparently popular among all his flock – Irish, Norman and Scandinavian. In 1180, he travelled to Normandy in France to seek a meeting with Henry II but was taken ill and died in the house of the Canons Regular of St Augustine, at Eu, on November 14th. His remains lie buried at Eu but his heart, enclosed in a casket, is supposedly preserved at Christ Church Cathedral in Dublin. Laurence was canonised in 1225.

During the 14th century, the settlement went into decline and lost much of its former glory but it seems to have still been important enough in 1398 for the Annals to record its destruction that summer by the English. The diocese of Glendalough was re-established by the Pope, about 1450, with bishops acceptable to the local inhabitants. The last of these bishops, one Denis White, a Dominican friar, surrendered to the Archbishop of Dublin in 1497. Abbots continued to be appointed up until the general supression of the monasteries under Henry VIII.

A Place of Pilgrimage

Glendalough was, from the time of St Kevin, a great centre of pilgrimage. This is evident from the references in the Annals and the 'Lives' of St Kevin already mentioned. Even after the supression of the monastery it is clear that the pattern of pilgrimage continued to be an important annual event celebrated on the feast day of St Kevin, June 3rd. The word pattern is derived from the Irish word *pátrún* meaning patron saint and refers to the celebration of the feast day of the local saint. While the pilgrimage at Glendalough, in the centuries after Kevin's death, was most likely a purely religious event, it had by at least the 18th century become a folk festival celebrated with the usual trappings associated with any traditional secular gathering.

The religious aspect of the pattern involved walking around the valley visiting the various churches, the station crosses and the holy well. Once the acts of devotion had been performed, the celebration proper began. A report from the year 1714 tells of how the pattern had degenerated into a riotous assembly. The high sheriff, in an attempt to supress the devotions of the papists at St Kevin's shrine, raised a posse. The said posse arrived in Glendalough at four o'clock on the morning of June 3rd. They pulled down the pilgrims' tents, destroyed their crosses and filled up their wells. While this may have affected the pattern in that year, it certainly did not affect it in the long term.

No less than three fine paintings depicting the pattern at Glendalough survive from the early 19th century. Two are by Maria Spilsbury Taylor, while the third is by Joseph Peacock. The painting by Peacock depicts the pattern in 1813 and is perhaps the most valuable with regard to the depiction of the celebrations. It clearly shows how the pilgrimage had become a kind of folk festival, resembling a fairground with its various

sideshows. We see a crowded ale-house as well as various dealers selling hardware, hats, shoes, toys, oranges and a variety of other food items. There are gaming tables, men playing skittles, a ballad singer and even a blind fiddler. Faction fighting was a common occurence at such events and a large mob armed with sticks is seen rushing across the scene scattering people in all directions.

Sir William Wilde, father of Oscar Wilde, writing in 1873, says that he had often attended the pattern staying there until the mid-afternoon, at which time the faction fights tended to begin and the place became quite unsafe. He tells us that while pilgrims performed the rounds, there was dancing, drinking, thimble-rigging and other amusements taking place. He adds that some twenty years earlier, the then parish priest banned the pattern and that it ceased to be celebrated.

Glendalough was linked to West Wicklow by a pilgrimage road which probably started at Hollywood. While most of the road has now disappeared, exposed sections of it can still be seen. Part of the road, near the Wicklow Gap, was excavated in 1972 and revealed a stone pavement over 3 metres wide, partially raised above the surrounding boggy land. A number of cross-inscribed or decorated stones were located at points along its route.

Saint Kevin in Legend

Glendalough, at one time Leinster's most important place of pilgrimage, is steeped in folk tradition. The greater part of this lore revolves around St Kevin, the patron saint and founder of Glendalough.

The various 'Lives' of St Kevin contain a great number of legends and miracles, many of which can be paralleled in folk tradition. During the 18th and 19th centuries, Glendalough attracted many tourists and travellers some of whom wrote accounts of their visits. Some of these writers describe in detail the legends associated with the gloomy valley while others allude to them. Among the many legends and stories told about St Kevin, are a collection of tales which deal with the animals and birds he loved so much. Of the dozens of different legends concerning Kevin, the following are among the more popular.

St Kevin and the Blackbird

Kevin was especially fond of birds and when he lived at Glendalough, the birds used to eat from his hands and perch on the top of his head. One day while praying near Reefert Church, close to the Upper Lake, with his arms outstretched in the form of a cross, a blackbird landed on his arm and laid its eggs in one of his hands. Kevin was so moved by this that he kept his arms outstretched until the eggs were hatched. This explains why St Kevin is often portrayed holding a blackbird in his hand. A 12th century illustration of Kevin shows him seated in a chair with the blackbird perched on the palm of his hand.

Saint Kevin and the Lark

Beloved as the blackbird was to the Saint, the lark was seemingly not so fortunate. Another legend explains why, according to tradition, the lark is never seen or heard at Glendalough. King O'Toole, the local chieftain, had some men working for him and the agreement which he made with them was that they would get up with the lark and go to bed with the lamb. The men could not stand these long hours and they went to the saint to implore his help. Kevin listened to their story and decided to banish the lark from Glendalough forever. Since then, the lark has never been seen at Glendalough.

King O'Toole's Goose

King O'Toole also features in a legend about a goose. Seemingly, when St Kevin first came to Glendalough, he was on the lookout for a piece of land on which to build a church.

One day as he walked along the road, he met King O'Toole who seemed to be quite upset. Upon asking him what was wrong, the King told Kevin that his pet gander, which had been given to him by his mother, was very ill and could not be cured. Kevin said that he would cure the goose if the King agreed to give him as much land as it would fly around. The King, not realising that Kevin was a saint, immediately agreed. Kevin blessed the gander and threw it up into the air to fly. The gander circled round the entire valley of Glendalough and Kevin claimed his just reward.

The Deer Stone is located beside the foot bridge over the Glenealo River, not very far from St Kevin's Church or 'Kitchen'. This is a large block of granite with a small basin carved in it and is a bullaun stone. Such stones were possibly used by the monks for grinding herbs or cereals. It is said to have got its name during the time of St Kevin when he was building the churches.

One day, the wife of one of the workmen died while giving birth to twins. The father was unable to look after the babies and he brought them to the monastery to be cared for. Unfortunately, the monks had no milk to give them either and they went to the saint to seek his advice. Kevin prayed to God and the next morning a wild hind came down from Derrybawn Mountain and allowed him to milk it into the hollow in the stone. The deer returned every morning until the babies were weaned.

St Kevin and Kathleen

The most celebrated of all the legends concerning St Kevin is the one about a girl called Kathleen. According to one version of the tale, the beautiful Kathleen fell in love with Kevin and followed him to Glendalough.

One night as Kevin was asleep in his bed, a cave in the cliffs above the Upper Lake, he had a dream in which he saw Kathleen standing between him and the gates of heaven. When he awoke, he realised that Kathleen had climbed up to the cave and was bending over him staring into his face. Kevin was overcome with rage and he dragged the girl to the entrance of the cave and flung her down the cliff to a watery grave in the lake below.

Some people remove all blame from the saint by explaining that Kathleen was not a real woman but Satan in disguise. Another version of the story tells how Kevin chastised the girl with a bunch of stinging nettles. This seems to have cooled her ardour for she fell at the saint's feet and begged his forgiveness. She was so sorry, we are told, that she entered a nunnery and devoted the rest of her life to God.

The Loaves of Bread

Kevin was very charitable and he disliked greedy people. One day as he was walking along the Green Road, he met a woman with an apron full of loaves of bread. She said to herself that if Kevin asked her for some bread, she would tell him that they were stones that she had. Kevin knew what was in her mind, so he stopped her and asked for some bread. The woman said that all she had was an apron full of stones. Kevin looked at her and said, 'If they are stones may they become bread, but if they are bread may they become stones'. The loaves of bread immediately turned into stones and were so heavy that they fell through her apron onto the side of the road.

The large stones, shaped like loaves, were to be seen along the Green Road for many years as a reminder to greedy people to be more charitable. Unfortunately, they have disappeared in more recent times.

Monuments to the East of the Lakes

The Gateway

The stream which flows in front of the ancient gateway is the Glendasan River which takes its name from the neighbouring Glendasan Valley through which it flows. A little further downstream, it joins the Glenealo River and then just to the south of Laragh it joins the Avonmore River. A bridge dating from the middle of the 19th century crosses the stream. Earlier drawings and paintings of the site show a ford and stepping stones.

The ancient gateway to the monastic City of Glendalough is one of the most important monuments in the valley as it is totally unique in Ireland. Formerly, other ecclesiastical sites such as Clonmacnoise in Offaly and Kells in Meath may well have had similar entrance gates but no traces of these structures have survived.

The building at Glendalough probably dates from the 11th or early 12th centuries and may have been built on the site of an earlier wooden structure. It is almost square in shape and measures 4.8 x 4.9 metres on the inside. The two large arches in the north and south walls are built of blocks of wrought granite. The arches are quite plain with no form of decoration.

The walls which connect the arches to the east and west are composed for the most part of mica-schist. The antae or projections, used to support the end beams of the roof, at the four outer corners of the building are typical of 10th and 11th-century church architecture. The gateway originally had an upper floor which would have been used as a gatekeeper's residence.

On the right hand side, just inside the gateway, is a large slab of mica-schist on which is a finely incised cross with an interesting, curved shaft. This is the sanctuary cross and it marked the boundary of church law. Any person who had committed a crime outside of the eccliastical settlement could enter and seek sanctuary or protection inside the enclosure.

The steps up to the gateway are modern and lead to the sloping path or causeway which is partly composed of ancient paving slabs. The causeway leads directly to the main ecclesiastical enclosure, which now contains a graveyard which has been used by people from the locality since the 16th century. A modern extension to this graveyard is located to the west of the Round Tower.

The Round Tower

Round Towers are peculiarly Irish and there are the remains of some 65 such buildings in the country. Some are well preserved like this one at Glendalough while others survive in a fragmentary state. Round Towers, a common feature of early Irish monasteries, were built between the 10th and 12th centuries and had a number of uses. Their Irish name *Cloigtheach*, meaning bell-tower, suggests their main use. However, these towers were also used as storehouses where the manuscripts and other monastic treasures were placed for safe keeping when the ecclesiastical settlement was threatened by hostile forces. They also served both as lookout posts and as beacons for approaching monks and pilgrims.

The Glendalough Round Tower, which is one of the finest surviving examples, is built of stone and mortar. Composed chiefly of mica-schist, interspersed with blocks of granite, it stands 30 metres above the present ground level. The foundation which is just one metre deep rests on a gravel subsoil and is continuous under the whole tower. The lower part of the tower has an external diameter of 4.9 metres and an internal diameter of 2.7 metres.

The doorway to the tower faces south-east towards the Cathedral. It is 3.5 metres above the ground and was reached by ladder. The sides of the doorway are inclined and the top is formed by a monolithic arch, cut from a single stone. The stones comprising the doorway are, for the most part, granite and are the full thickness of the wall. The position of the doorway, so high up, may have been for security, both for protecting the valuables stored there or maybe even the monks themselves in times of attack.

The tower originally had six wooden floors resting on beams set into the wall, making seven storeys in all. The storey below the doorway has no window while the four floors above the door are all lit by one small window. The top floor has four windows, larger than the lower ones and almost in line with the cardinal compass points.

The cap or roof of the tower is conical in shape and is built using the corbelling technique. It is finished by using a conical capstone at the top. Many old drawings of Glendalough show the tower without its conical cap, which was hit by lightning sometime during the 17th century and collapsed into the tower. It was rebuilt in 1876 by the Office of Public Works using the stones which had been found lying inside.

The Cathedral

The Cathedral which is situated 43 metres to the south-east of the Round Tower, is the largest and most prominent church at Glendalough. It was dedicated to St Peter and St Paul but ceased to be a cathedral when the diocese of Glendalough was united with that of Dublin in 1214. The building consists of two main phases of construction. The nave is from the first period while the chancel, sacristy and north doorway are from the second. The nave, which measures 14.6 x 9.1 metres internally, is the widest surviving pre-Romanesque church in Ireland. It incorporates the large stones and other features of an earlier stone church. This was fully removed to make way for the nave of the present building which appears to have been built in the 10th century.

The nave has antae projecting both east and west from the side walls and these provided a broad base for the heavy end beams of the roof. The masonry of the nave is of two kinds. The lower parts of the walls (about 2 metres in height in the west and about 1 metre in the side walls) are in Cyclopean masonry, using large slabs of mica-schist laid on edge to form a relatively thin facing, to a rubble core. The upper portions of the walls are built in uncoursed rubble consisting of smaller and rougher stones. The west doorway is lintelled and has, above the lintel, a round relieving arch, the full thickness of the wall. There are two windows in the south wall.

The chancel, which measures 11.3 x 6.7 metres internally, was built in the 12th century. The remains of the chancel arch are decorated with chevron motifs and angle mouldings. The large east window which is round-headed and splays widely inwards has been completely reconstructed with most of the original wrought stones. The head of the window is also decorated with chevron motifs. The stone used in the construction of the east window, the chancel arch and the north doorway is not local in origin, nor is it Irish. It is in fact an oolitic limestone which was imported from the Dundry quarries near Bristol in England. This type of stone, popular among masons in Ireland, during the late 12th century, was also used in a number of buildings in Dublin. Its use in this building is an indication of the prosperity of the monastery towards the end of the 12th century.

Under the south window are the remains of an aumbry or wall cupboard where the sacred vessels for Mass were stored and a recess with a basin, called a piscina, was used for washing the vessels after they had been used. A doorway in the south wall opens into the small sacristy.

Saint Kevin's Cross

   Just south of the cathedral is the large undecorated cross known as St Kevin's Cross. This monolith of granite stands 3.7 metres high and is a Celtic cross with the characteristic ring or circle around the arms. The ring is slightly sunk on both sides but not perforated. Limited excavations were carried out in 1989 around the base of the cross to straighten and consolidate it. These excavations revealed a stone base worked from a large granite boulder which is visible today. The upper part of the base was smoothed to give a rectangular surface with a central socket for the cross shaft.

   From here, part of the original boundary wall of an earlier cemetery can be traced. The enclosure measured some 30 metres in length from east to west and 22 metres from north to south. Traces of the wall can still be seen to the south of St Kevin's Cross but the best preserved portion lies to the north-east of the enclosure where almost half of it survives.

The Priests' House

To the west of St Kevin's Cross and within the boundary of the ancient cemetery lies a small building known as the Priests' House. The name 'Priests' House' derives from an 18th century practice of burying Catholic priests in the floor of the building. According to local folk tradition, the clay from the floor of the building held a cure for toothache. The clay was simply rubbed on the jaw in order to gain relief.

This building was in a very ruinous condition when it was taken into State care in 1869. Except for the lower parts of the walls, the present structure is a reconstruction carried out in the 1870s using original stones and based on drawings made by Beranger on his visit to Glendalough in 1779. The reconstruction, which may not be totally accurate, has been the subject of much debate among architectural historians.

This small structure measures 4.47 x 2.36 metres internally. There is a narrow doorway in the south wall. Inside the building, there is a recess in the west wall and a number of headstones which commemorate some of the priests who are buried there. The most important feature of the building lies to the east where there is a recess with a decorative Romanesque arch which is partially filled in by a wall leaving a narrow window opening. The decoration consists mainly of chevron patterns and angular beads. The drawings made by Beranger also depict human faces with interlaced hair but unfortunately these do not survive.

Above the doorway of the building and acting as a lintel, is part of an interesting carving which has been interpreted as representing an ecclesiastic, seated between two figures. The figure on the left bears a crozier while the one on the right carries a bell. The carving is incomplete and also badly weathered, but the figure carrying the bell is clearly visible. There is no evidence to suggest that this stone was originally a lintel but was placed in its present position during the reconstruction work of the 1870s.

The original use of the building is uncertain. It may have been erected over the grave of Kevin himself or have housed some relics of the saint. If this is so, then the purpose of the narrow window may have been to allow pilgrims to peer inside at the grave or relics, yet prevent them from actually entering the shrine.

Saint Kevin's Church or 'Kitchen'

To the south of St Kevin's Cross and located on slightly lower ground is St Kevin's – Glendalough's most famous and best loved church. The building is popularly known as 'St Kevin's Kitchen', as the belfry rising from the west gable is said to resemble a chimney. The structure comprises a nave with a later sacristy and chancel added to the east. Only the foundation of the chancel survives. It was during a later period of building that the chancel arch was cut through the original east wall of the nave and this is now used as the entrance.

The original church is rectangular in shape and measures 6.91 x 4.45 metres internally. The walls are 1.17 metres thick and slope very slightly inwards both inside and outside. The masonry is mainly of mica-schist but a small amount of granite was also used.

The original entrance is to the west. This doorway is trabeate (of post and lintel construction rather than an arch) and like the Cathedral, it has a relieving arch above the massive lintel. The lintel, which extends right through the wall, is of mica-schist and has a hood projecting from it. This hood has two holes worked in it which were used for securing a timber door. The doorway narrows slightly from floor level to lintel. Originally, there was a narrow window in the south wall of the church. This window was enlarged during the early 19th century when, for a number of years from

about 1810, St Kevin's Church was in regular use as a Catholic church for the local population. However, because the ground legally belonged to the Church of Ireland, the Catholic archbishop was forced to order that its use as a chapel be discontinued.

The extent of this window, which was subsequently blocked up, can be seen on the inside of the building. Another window existed in the east wall. This round headed window was filled in when the chancel arch was opened up but its top can still be discerned above the arch. Externally, there is a projecting string or eaves course all around the building.

Internally, there was a wooden floor 3.8 metres above ground level which created a first floor chamber between the church and the croft or chamber in the roof space. Some of the beam holes can still be seen in the interior walls. This chamber, lit by a single square headed window in the east gable may have provided accommodation for a priest or monk. However, when the later chancel was added to the building, the small window would have opened into the croft of the chancel thus blocking off the light.

The most interesting feature of the building is the steep stone roof. It is formed of overlapping stones on the corbel principle with each stone sloping slightly outwards to deter the entry of rainwater. On the interior, a true arch of rough masonry is introduced creating a nearly semi-circular vault which also strengthens the roof slopes at their weakest point. Above the arch is a croft or attic space, which may have been used as an apartment, the entrance to which is through a rectangular opening towards the

western end of the vault. The croft is lit by a small square headed window in the east gable. The roof structure can be compared with that of St Columba's House, Kells, Co. Meath and Cormac's Chapel, Cashel, Co. Tipperary.

A very striking feature of the building is the belfry which is in the form of a miniature round tower. It rises from the west gable and adjoining roof, tapering very slightly. The tower, an original feature of the building, is three storeys in height and has an internal diameter of just over a metre at the bottom. The lower part is lit by a small window to the west, above which is another to the east, while the top is lit by four larger windows, facing approximately towards the cardinal compass points. The conical roof is built on the corbel principle and a narrow eaves course projects slightly from its base. Some scholars have suggested that the tower may have been a later addition to the building while others argue that it is an original feature.

The church was altered at a later date with the addition of a chancel and a sacristy to the east. Both had corbelled stone roofs with small crofts. The line of the chancel roof is marked by the groove in the face of the nave wall and the foundations of its walls can be seen in the ground to the east. A drawing in the Royal Irish Academy, possibly by Beranger (1779), shows the chancel standing. While it is not clear exactly when it collapsed, or was demolished, it is generally agreed that it disappeared during the early part of the 19th century.

Saint Kieran's Church

To the south-east of St Kevin's Church lie the remains of St Kieran's, the smallest of the surviving churches at Glendalough. This church, with coeval nave and chancel, was discovered beneath a mound of earth and stones in 1875. Only the foundation and about half a metre of the superstructure remain. The nave measures 5.7 x 4.4 metres internally and the chancel is 2.8 x 2.7 metres. The west doorway is built of large stones resting on a granite sill. The foundation of a stone altar was discovered in the chancel and there is a small doorway in its south wall. This doorway probably led to a sacristy of which all other traces have disappeared.

It has been suggested that this little church was erected in honour of St Kieran of Clonmacnoise who died around the middle of the 6th century. The present building is possibly no earlier than 11th century.

Saint Mary's Church

St Mary's or Our Lady's Church is located a short distance to the west of the main enclosure. It consists of a nave with a later, possibly 12th century, chancel. The nave measures 9.8 metres in length internally and narrows from 6.1 metres in width at the west to 5.9 metres at the east. The most important feature of this church is its massive west doorway. Its sill and lintel are each composed of a single stone. The jamb at each side is formed of three blocks of granite which extend through the entire thickness of the wall. Around the outside of the doorway is a slightly raised architrave or frame and upon the soffit or underside of the lintel is an incised saltire cross with circular expansions at the centre and ends of the arms. Above the doorway is a string course. There is one small window high up in the south wall of the nave which is round-headed and splayed and has a small hood moulding. The door in the north wall is a later addition.

The chancel, which is not bonded into the wall of the nave, is built in masonry which is of much poorer quality. It measures 6.2 x 5.4 metres internally. The east window is round-headed and has a hood moulding decorated with a key pattern and ending in animal heads which are almost worn away. It contains the base of an altar on which is placed a bullaun stone. Two early Christian memorial slabs can be seen in the chancel and a third one lies outside the south wall. There are some interesting upright cross slabs in the burial ground surrounding the church.

Trinity Church

This little church is located beside the main road to the east of the main enclosure. It has sometimes been called 'Ivy Church' because of the former profuse growth of that plant on its walls. It is a coeval nave and chancel church with a very fine granite chancel arch. A small annexe was later added to the west of the building and this supported a belfry. The nave measures 9 x 5.3 metres internally. The original doorway is to the west and is lintelled with sloping jambs. When the annexe was added, the west doorway opened into it and a new round-headed doorway was constructed in the south wall of the nave. There is also a small round-headed window in the south wall. The chancel measures 4.1 x 2.7 metres internally and has two small windows. The semi-circular-headed east window with its external projecting hood is cut from a single stone. The south window is unusual as it has an angular head formed of two flat stones and is the only specimen of this kind surviving at Glendalough. The chancel arch is composed of fifteen dressed granite stones and spans the full width of the chancel, resting on the corners of the walls. Externally, there are six projecting corbels at the gables of the nave and chancel which would have carried the verge timbers of the roof. The annexe to the west may have been used as a sacristy. A round tower or belfry was constructed over a vault in this chamber. There are a number of drawings in existence which show this tower before it was blown down during a storm in 1818. Some of the corbelling of the roof of the annexe still survives. That on the north wall is original while that on the south wall was reconstructed in 1875. It has been estimated that the tower would have been some 18 metres in height.

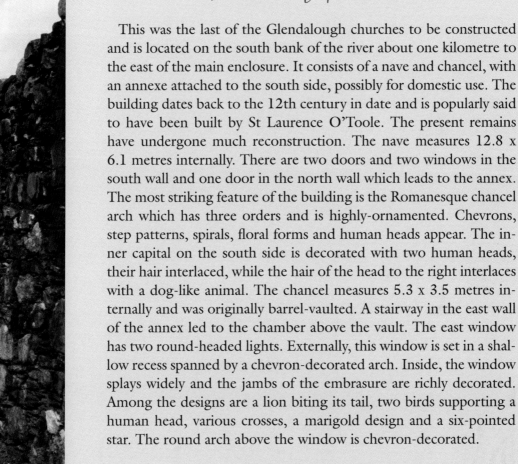

The Monastery of Saint Saviour

This was the last of the Glendalough churches to be constructed and is located on the south bank of the river about one kilometre to the east of the main enclosure. It consists of a nave and chancel, with an annexe attached to the south side, possibly for domestic use. The building dates back to the 12th century in date and is popularly said to have been built by St Laurence O'Toole. The present remains have undergone much reconstruction. The nave measures 12.8 x 6.1 metres internally. There are two doors and two windows in the south wall and one door in the north wall which leads to the annex. The most striking feature of the building is the Romanesque chancel arch which has three orders and is highly-ornamented. Chevrons, step patterns, spirals, floral forms and human heads appear. The inner capital on the south side is decorated with two human heads, their hair interlaced, while the hair of the head to the right interlaces with a dog-like animal. The chancel measures 5.3 x 3.5 metres internally and was originally barrel-vaulted. A stairway in the east wall of the annex led to the chamber above the vault. The east window has two round-headed lights. Externally, this window is set in a shallow recess spanned by a chevron-decorated arch. Inside, the window splays widely and the jambs of the embrasure are richly decorated. Among the designs are a lion biting its tail, two birds supporting a human head, various crosses, a marigold design and a six-pointed star. The round arch above the window is chevron-decorated.

The Market Cross

This granite cross which once stood in the old market place opposite the local hotel is now preserved in the Visitor Centre. It measures 1.7 metres in height. The cross has no ring but the billets at the angles of the arms indicate that the design is derived from the ringed type. On the front is carved, in high relief, a crucifixion scene. The figure of Christ wears a garment to the knees, while the head is crowned and inclined. Below this is a figure, possibly a bishop. Two small figures can also be made out on the front of the base. The back of the cross has a floral pattern on the head and zoomorphic or animal-based interlacings on the shaft.

The Market Cross belongs to a group of 12th century crosses which differ greatly from the earlier scripture crosses. The crucifixion scene and the figure of a bishop or saint both in high relief have replaced the biblical scenes of this earlier type, and the shafts tend to be decorated with interlace and animal patterns. showing a strong Scandinavian influence. Other examples of this style of cross are at Tuam, Co. Galway, Roscrea, Co. Tipperary and at Dysert O'Dea and Kilfenora Co. Clare.

Temple-na-Skellig

This church stands on a shelf about 6 metres above the southern shore of the Upper Lake and is almost impossible and highly dangerous to access except by boat. A series of rough steps lead from the landing place to the small rectangular church which measures 7.6 x 4.3 metres internally. The granite doorway has inclined jambs and the massive lintel lies nearby. The church appears to date from the 11th or 12th century. The east window dates from the later period. This would appear to be the site which the Latin 'Life' refers to when it records that a church was built by Kevin's followers between the lake and mountain where Kevin had his hermitage. To the west of the church is a raised platform with stone enclosure walls. This area was excavated in the late 1950s and revealed wattle huts connected by paved paths. At a later date, a wooden house was erected in the middle of the platform.

Saint Kevin's Bed

This man-made cave is situated in the rock face to the east of Temple-na-Skellig, about 9 metres above the level of the lake. It runs back 2 metres into the rock and is less than a metre high and wide. This cave was supposedly used by St Kevin and later by St Laurence O'Toole as a retreat during the season of Lent. It has been associated in more recent times with the legend of Kathleen.

A visit to St Kevin's Bed formed part of the pilgrimage to the valley and according to popular tradition, pregnant women climbed into the Bed in order to ensure a safe delivery. Access to the Bed was by boat and then up a flight of rough steps.

Saint Kevin's Cell

This structure was built on a rocky spur overlooking Reefert Church but only the foundation of it remains today. It was a circular hut, 3.6 metres in diameter with walls 0.9 metres thick. It had a doorway facing east. It was possibly a beehive hut, roofed in stone and corbelled, and might have resembled those at the island monastery of Skellig Michael, Co. Kerry.

Reefert Church

This little church with coeval nave and chancel closely resembles Trinity Church in style. It is situated in a grove of hazel trees to the south-east of the Upper Lake. The nave measures 8.9 x 5.9 metres internally. It has a trabeate doorway (of post and lintel construction rather than an arch) with sloping jambs. There are two round-headed windows in the south wall. The chancel arch is of well-cut granite and spans the width of the chancel which measures 4 x 2.4 metres internally and has a small round-headed window to the east. Outside, there are a total of six projecting corbels, one at each gable, and these carried the verge timbers for the roof. Originally, there was a stone-walled enclosure or cashel around the church and graveyard but this has disappeared. The present enclosing walls and terracing date from 1875.

The name Reefert is derived from *Rígh Fearta* meaning the burial place of the kings and is popularly associated with the O'Toole clan. This, however, may be purely as a result of the misreading of a memorial slab in the late 18th century which is supposed to have referred to King O'Toole. Another scholar, some years later, showed the reading of the inscription to be Or do Carpre 'Mac Cathuill' meaning 'A prayer for Carpre son of Cathall'. The O'Tooles moved into this mountainous region in the latter part of the 12th century when they were ousted from their lands in Kildare by the Normans.

The Caher

To the east of the Upper Lake are the remains of a stone enclosure, 20 metres in diameter. Although of unknown date, some scholars describe it as a fort and see it as evidence of an early occupation of the valley. Two such enclosures were noted in 1839 and it was suggested that they were not forts but more likely enclosures for cattle. More recently, it has been suggested that they may have served as meeting places or shelters for pilgrims. Several small crosses can be seen in the area of the 'Caher'. These may have marked stations on the pilgrim's route around the valley.